SELECTIONS from

MW00368459

A piano accompaniment book (HL00841182) is available for this collection.

ISBN 0-7935-8037-4

7777 W. BLUEMOUND RD. P.O. BOX 13819 MILWAUKEE, WI 53213

Visit Hal Leonard Online at
www.halleonard.com

JELLICLE SONGS FOR JELLICLE CATS

Music by ANDREW LLOYD WEBBER

Text by TREVOR NUNN and RICHARD STILGOE after T.S. ELIOT

Violin

Mysteriously, freely

Rhythmic

Light Rock

3

Growing intensity

THE OLD GUMBIE CAT

Violin

Music by ANDREW LLOYD WEBBER
Text by T.S. ELIOT

Thoughtfully, moderate

Bright Swing feel

BUSTOPHER JONES: THE CAT ABOUT TOWN

Music by ANDREW LLOYD WEBBER
Text by T.S. ELIOT

Violin

OLD DEUTERONOMY

Music by ANDREW LLOYD WEBBER
Text by T.S. ELIOT

Violin

GUS: THE THEATRE CAT

Music by ANDREW LLOYD WEBBER
Text by T.S. ELIOT

Violin

MR. MISTOFFELEES

Music by ANDREW LLOYD WEBBER
Text by T.S. ELIOT

Violin

SKIMBLESHANKS: THE RAILWAY CAT

Music by ANDREW LLOYD WEBBER
Text by T.S. ELIOT

Violin

MEMORY

Violin

Music by ANDREW LLOYD WEBBER
Text by TREVOR NUNN after T.S. ELIOT

THE AD-DRESSING OF CATS

Music by ANDREW LLOYD WEBBER
Text by T.S. ELIOT

Violin

THE JOURNEY TO THE HEAVYSIDE LAYER

Violin

Music by ANDREW LLOYD WEBBER
Text by T.S. ELIOT